FOCUS ON GOD

RATHER THAN MATERIALISTIC THINGS

Reviving yourself to change your world.

Second Edition

FOCUS ON GOD

RATHER THAN MATERIALISTIC THINGS

Reviving yourself to change your world.

Second Edition

Dr. Michael Andam

CreateSpace

Copyright © 2018 by Dr. Michael Andam
All rights reserved

First Published 2006 by Xulon Publishers
Second Edition 2018 by CreateSpace

This book or parts thereof may not be reproduced or transmitted in any form or by any means, electronic, mechanical, photography, recording, or by any information storage or retrieval system, without permission in writing from the publisher or Copyright House UK.

Unless otherwise noted, all Scripture quotations are from the New King James Version of the Bible. Copyright © 1979, 1980, 1982 by Thomas Nelson, Inc., publishers.

Cover design by Rachel Halili
Website: www.rachelhalili.com

Lovingly dedicated to my dearest
 Wife, Dorcas, a woman of great faith.

CONTENTS

Introduction 9
Chapter 1 The Primary Focus 11
Chapter 2 Focus and Vision 17
Chapter 3   Refocusing on Jesus 29
Chapter 4   Results of focusing on Jesus 39
Chapter 5   Focus on relationship 49
Chapter 6   The Faith Journey 61
Chapter 7   God's Awesome Presence 69
Chapter 8   How to Impact World 83
Chapter 9   Focus on Jesus-Change your World 97
Reference 105

Introduction.

I believe everyone who truly claim and live as a child of God (Christian) aim to finally make it to heaven. On the other hand, Jesus is not expecting us to show up alone in heaven. He wants us to share the good news of His kingdom with our brothers, sisters, relatives and in fact everybody. He wants all to come to heaven.

After Jesus' resurrection from the dead, He gave His power and authority to us for one purpose. It was for the church to share the greatest news of salvation to all mankind. "All authority has been given to Me in heaven and on earth. Go therefore and make disciples of all nations, baptizing them in the name of the Father and of the Son and of the Holy Spirit. Teaching them to observe all things that I have commanded you; and lo, I am with you always, even to the end of the age. Amen."

Over the years, the church seems to be doing everything else apart from fulfilling the main purpose in the above commission. Our world is indeed full of evil and that is not getting better. There are many things happening which the church can have great influence taking into consideration what Christ has already done. We have been talking for so long and quoting scriptures about who we are, but without any action. We say we are the light of the world, but we don't seem to influence anything in the society.

We have all the answers to our world's problems yet we are crying with the politicians and family on how bad things look like. It is about time to wake up the sleeping giant now to influence and change our world. It is time to practice what we have bee talking about for so many years.

Jesus demonstrated before teaching about what He did.

We also need to prepare ourselves and demonstrate the life of Jesus before we can be counted as His true witnesses. This is what this book aims to do. In studying this book you will discover and learn the following:

1. Where your primary focus as a child of God should be.
2. What have been done for you and what you need to do to get your focus right.
3. How to build a strong relationship with Jesus and enjoy His awesome presence daily.
4. How to make the study and reading of your Bible your top priority.
5. Walking our talk by living the lifestyle of Jesus and finally talking to people about Jesus. It is packed with many other teachings to equip the body of Christ for action in this 21st century.

-Chapter 1-

The Primary Focus

"......looking unto Jesus, the author and finisher of *our* faith.."Heb 12:1b. "But seek first the kingdom of God and His righteousness, and all these things shall be added to you."-Matthew 6:33

Explaining 'focus'
"Focus" is a very powerful word. The dictionary explains this as the center of activity, an act of concentrating interest or activity on something and finally to pay particular attention to something.

What is the focal point of your life? What do you pay particular attention to? How does this influence your life? From the explanation given, I believe it will be essential to apply this concept to all areas of our lives. It is also crucial for us to be focused on everything we do, such as in education, business and most importantly our spiritual lives.

For the purpose of this book, we will look at focusing on Jesus Christ as we read from part of the scriptures above. We will also discuss the results on focusing our lives on Him and how that can impact our society positively. The theme will be based on faith in Jesus (God) rooted in His Love.

We will first consider some few real life examples of the importance of how focusing on tasks plays in our daily lives.

As with all professionals, Pilots need great full concentration and focus throughout their flight. I believe it is one of the reasons they always have more than one in the cockpit. You can imagine the outcome if pilots about to take off or land their plane takes their eyes off the instruments or fail to pay attention to what the control tower is communicating to them?

Other examples that require deep concentration and focus will include a surgeon operating on a patient, a midwife delivering a baby, driving of a car or any vehicle, cooking, walking, working with factory machinery and in fact every aspect of our day to day activities.

The process in focusing means a demand in mental action of concentration. We engage our brain and other senses in practicing this. Some scientific experiments makes 'focus' more real.

The concept of focus-Jesus
"Therefore we also, since we are surrounded by so great a cloud of witnesses, let us lay aside every weight, and the sin which so easily ensnares *us,* and let us run with endurance the race that is set before us, looking unto Jesus, the author and finisher of our faith, who for the joy that was set before Him endured the cross, despising the shame, and has sat down at the right hand of the throne of God."-Heb 12:1-2

In the above scripture verse, we are encouraged to lay aside all forms of weight that comes with living the life that we have been given. The reason been that, such life distractions takes our focus off God and unfortunately put it on these temporal and less important negatives and finally robs us from enjoying God's rewards that comes with obedience and absolute faith in His word.

The beauty of this is the direction given to us to focus on Jesus who is the author and finisher of our faith. That is the big picture! Jesus is the center of life and everything. We are encouraged and at the same time taught on what to do in this faith journey.

Jesus is like a lighthouse where we can focus life and be assured not to have a 'shipwreck' of it. Is He in your life? Which part of your life have you allowed Him to be? We will explore more.

The verse also assured us that; Jesus set an example to endure the shame and painful death on the cross to set us free from sin and death.

Joshua's drawn line of focus

In the Bible, there was a leader called Joshua who God chose to succeed Moses to lead the people of Israel. Prior to his leadership, he was Moses' assistant and he had witnessed the character and conduct of his people for many years. One of the areas was that the people of Israel many a time did not concentrate on serving God alone and they drifted by serving idols, which was an abomination to God.

Joshua challenged them and helped to establish true worship by making worshiping God Almighty the only focal point of their lives. This was his challenge to them and I believe looking at our current world it should also apply to us:

> "Now therefore, fear the Lord, serve Him in sincerity and in truth, and put away the gods which your fathers served on the other side of the River and in Egypt. Serve the Lord!
> And if it seems evil to you to serve the Lord, choose for yourselves this day whom you will serve, whether the gods which your fathers served that were on the other side of the River, or the gods of the Amorites, in whose land you dwell. But as for me and my house, we will serve the Lord."-Joshua 24:14-15.

Joshua's challenge resonates in our time as we have more modern gods to worship maybe than in his time.

We now have various cults that promote secularism or Satanism, gadgets, celebrities and even ourselves to worship instead of God, especially the western world. What Joshua did was to put an end to what he witnessed during the time of his predecessor Moses when the people continuously provoked God by worshipping other gods. He drew the line of focus once and for all.

Jesus' concept of focus

As God, Jesus encouraged His followers not to worry about the daily necessities of life that normally tend to cause us to worry and thus get distracted from our focal point in life, which was discussed earlier.

> "Therefore do not worry, saying, 'What shall we eat?' or 'What shall we drink?' or 'What shall we wear?' For after all these things the Gentiles seek. For your heavenly Father knows that you need all these things. But **seek first the kingdom of God and His righteousness,** and all these things shall be added to you. Therefore do not worry about tomorrow, for tomorrow will worry about its own things. Sufficient for the day is its own trouble."- Mat 6:31-34

These are assuring words coming from the author of life. Jesus is asking us to focus on our primary goals, which are the kingdom of God and His righteousness. The promise for doing this is that all the other things that normally distract us will be given to us.

Theory verses Personal Practice

When I was about nine years old, my uncle bought me a magnifying lens from London. I had no idea of its usefulness at the time.

It was not until I went to high school some years after that I learnt of its possible usefulness. On one sunny afternoon, we went to our physics laboratory to conduct an experiment on an aspect of light. We were dealing with the subject on "prism" and that seemed to be very interesting.

At one point, the teacher demonstrated how focusing the rays of the sun directly through the lens had the capability to draw its power. The heat it generated from the sun was powerful enough to ignite and burn a piece of paper.

Guess what, I remembered I had my own lens at home. I could not wait for that semester to complete. I practiced using my own lens to conduct the experiment demonstrated by my physics teacher.

I practiced it for some time until I got it right to ignite the paper. I also used it to magnify tiny writings and was quite amazed at this magnificent piece of instrument.

I realised that it is one thing to see someone demonstrating, but a completely different feeling when you have a first hand experience. Now I always remember the experiment I conducted and not only what my teacher did.

This is also true for having a personal relationship with Jesus Christ. It is not always good for someone telling you what He can do all the time when you have access to Him as well. You can experience this as well and get to know Who He is and what He has done for you and what He expects of you to do.

-Chapter 2-

Focus and Vision

"…..looking unto Jesus, the author and finisher of *our* faith.."Heb 12:1b

Focus and Light
I believe that focusing will be effective in the presence of light and vision. Vision has everything to do with light. Imagine planning to go somewhere, say shopping. You first have the route in your mind and when gifted to see visually, depend on your eyes to get there. Even in darkness, we switch on the light when available to guide us.

Without light, it could be quite difficult to find our way around. With our vision, we are able to concentrate on activities in our daily lives. Jesus was so right to say that His followers are the light of the world.

The point here is that Jesus is the 'Big Light of the world." He said, "I am **the** light of the world. He who follows me shall not walk in darkness, but have the light of life." –John 8:12

As His followers, we are the 'smaller' light in the world. We do not have any 'light' in us until we accept Jesus Christ.

Jesus' life then becomes the light that shines through us as we live and do what He asked us to do. This encourages us to follow what Jesus did and stands for.

We must demonstrate the characteristics of light as Jesus did. Our character should reflect His for all to know that we are indeed His disciples.
We must shine the glorious light of the kingdom of heaven wherever we go.

The world must know that we are the light and the ones who have the answers to its' problems. It is not a matter of picking and choosing which days to do so. It is the lifestyle of Jesus' followers. The question is that, do we have the answers? No, we do not, however God the Son has it all and we can provide it. Do people recognise you as the light in the light in the communities or an irrelevant religion? Have we lost our vision?

Focus on the Son-Jesus' Focus And Vision.
During His first mission to earth, Jesus had focus. Normally, at age 12, majority of children do not know exactly what they want to do in future. Some may even have two to three options.

At the age of 12, the Boy Jesus knew exactly what His vision and mission was. His parents went to Jerusalem every year as their custom to celebrate the feast of the Passover. During one of such celebrations, the parents realised that the Boy Jesus was not with them.

This was after they had travelled for a whole day.

They came back to Jerusalem and found Him sitting among the Jewish teachers listening and asking them questions. When the parents questioned Him of His action, He responded,

"Why did you seek Me? Did you not know that I must be about My Father's business?"-Luke 2:29

The gospel of Luke explains that the earthly parents of Jesus did not understand that statement. We are very privileged to understand His focus today. What was His Father's business? God's business is the salvation for everybody through His Son Jesus Christ. This has now become the believers of Christ's vision and mission as well. There is a scripture that brings this to light:

"For God so loved the world that He gave His only begotten Son, that whoever believes in Him should not perish but have everlasting life. For God did not send His Son into the world to condemn the world, but that the world through Him might be saved."-John 3:16-17

The Father's ultimate desire is for humanity to be saved through Jesus Christ His only Son. "Who desires that all men to be saved and to come to the knowledge of the truth (Jesus), for there is one God and One Mediator between God and men, the Man Christ Jesus, who gave Himself a ransom for all to be testified in due time." - 1Tim 2:4-5.

Jesus did not lost His focus at any point in His ministry. He never lost His vision and purpose. His focus was to go to the cross, die, and resurrect to pay for the price of our sin, which was the disobedience to God. He did not condemn the world but demonstrated His love for all. He loved the sinner, healed all the sick people, raised the dead, cleansed the lepers, and cast out demons.

Through this, He accomplished His mission and all humanity can now have eternal life in Christ Jesus when they accept Him as their only Saviour. This is an example of the importance of focus.

Two "faces" of Focus:
I call this the principle of "Walk" or "sink" effect as part of the my concept and perception of 'focus.'

The first part is what I describe as focus on Jesus and walk on water. After a hectic ministry to a large crowd Jesus asked His disciples to take the lead. They were by now in the middle of the sea when they saw someone coming, walking on the water. They were very much afraid. Well who wouldn't be! Jesus called out and quenched their fear. He came walking on the water!! Peter said to Him, "lord if it is you command me to come to You on the water"-Mat 14:28. The answer was "come on." Peter looked unto Jesus and stepped out of the boat and walked on the water to meet Jesus. What an experience for Peter and the other disciples!

Now here is the second part of what I describe as focus on "fear and sink' in the water: Unfortunately, Peter took his eyes off Jesus and focused on the raging waves of the sea. Faith disappeared and was replaced with fear. Peter immediately begun to sink. He called to Jesus for help. Jesus rebuked him for disbelief.

Indeed the work of salvation was completed. All men can be saved from the wrath that is to come on all the children of disobedience. Hell is not meant for any created person except Satan and the fallen angels. Let us literally focus on Jesus in everything we do and avoid sinking into depression and the others.

The Commission-Focus On Souls.

"And I also say to you that you are Peter, and on this rock I will build My church, and the gates of Hades shall not prevail against it."-Matthew 16:18.

Jesus established the church and said the gates of hell cannot prevail against it. He meant no evil can destroy the purpose for which the church exists.

There have been various types of persecution and lies to distract the church from the main focus to win lost souls for Christ. Before Jesus ascended to heaven, He commissioned all His followers, present and future to continue with His great work. What a privilege to know that angels were not given this assignment of salvation but to us.

Jesus said, "All authority has been given to Me in heaven and on earth.

Go therefore and make disciples of all the nations, baptizing them in the name of the Father and of the Son and of the Holy Spirit, teaching them to observe all things that I have commanded you: lo I am with you always, even to the end of the age." -Matthew 28: 18-20.

Jesus will not send us without equipping and providing for our needs both spiritual and physical. Jesus' vision and mission is a worldwide ministry of soul winning through teaching the good news of the kingdom of God. This is the first and foremost vision and mission for anyone who receives Jesus as their Saviour. This is now the great commission of the church, which is the body of Christ. Our focus must be the same as Jesus' and nothing else- sharing the good news with all lost souls.

This may sounds easy and straightforward. On the other hand, this seem to have become the great omission of the church with the same reasons given as Satan's attempts to distract.

We need to address this and go back to where Jesus wants us to be. Our vision should be the same as that of Jesus, to see all saved, as this cannot be over emphasized. Our mission is to tell the world about salvation in Christ Jesus.

This means that we should leave our comfort zones and go and tell others about Jesus. We have been equipped to do so.

We will later study the difference between authority and power and relate it to what the church has been given.

The Devil's Focus And Your Position.
The church has been warned about an enemy called Satan. We are so blessed to know that Jesus conquered him on the cross at Calvary. We are no longer under the power of sin and temptation. You stand at a better position in Christ because of what He did for you and not what you can do for Him by way of works, as some may believe.

> "And you, being dead in your trespasses and the uncircumcision of your flesh, He has made alive together with Him, having forgiven you all trespasses, having wiped out the handwriting of requirements that was against us, which was contrary to us. And He has taken it out of the way, having nailed it to the cross.
> Having disarmed principalities and powers, He made a public spectacle of them, triumphing over them in it." -Colossians 3:13-15

Although defeated, Satan is still in the world and causing havoc, but his final days are just around the corner. His number one desire remains the same. He still longs to be worshiped as god and will continue to do all he can to achieve this.

Satan's number one enemy is the Godhead, Father, Son and the Holy Spirit. The only Jesus he can focus his attack now are His followers.

Jesus' followers are part of His body, the church as we read earlier... I will build my church...

He will use all his deadly arsenals that Jesus warned us beforehand to distract our focus on winning souls for the kingdom of God. Some of these arsenals are causing many Christians to disobey Jesus by committing physical and spiritual adultery, lying to one another, envy and all evil deeds.

He knows his time is very short because Jesus is coming back soon. In view of this he is working very hard to cause many Christians to fall, using the same principle used in the Garden of Eden, which is twisting the word of God in such a way as to deceive. He is using some themes in films, false prophets and haters of Jesus to come up with doctrines of demons to distract Christians. Some may be so subtle that it may even deceive the elite Christian! If he is able to distract us from our main focus in life then he will succeed.

Our current position?

What is our present position? There are many good and great things happening in the body of Christ that is note worthy. People are still accepting the gospel of Jesus and many lives are being transformed all over the world. Many are totally focused on the great commission and seeing the impact of God's supernatural presence and power at work.

How do we measure performance? The world has their criteria of measuring performance. Our standard is based on our mission. So where are we now?

Although there are many good things happening, there are still some few things hindering the church from making greater impact. In the first edition we read some few practices that negatively impacted the church.

Over the last eleven years we have some few more practices that gravely negatively impact the church even more. I will list a few of the issues, which I believe is distracting the church from our main focus once again. You can look at your own congregation and see if these are present. I am not going to mention any names or churches, but you know where you stand.

Some problems facing the 21st century church:

1. Rise of Wolves. The apostle Paul warned the early church that a time will come when savage wolves will infiltrate the church. Paul's warning appears to be a process starting with the appearance of these wolves rising to what they intend to do. "For I have not shunned to declare to you the whole counsel of God. Therefore take heed to yourselves and to all the flock, among which the Holy Spirit has made you overseers, to shepherd the church of God which He purchased with His own blood. For I know this that after my departure savage wolves will come in among you, not sparing the flock. -Acts 20-27-29

2. Alternative Gospel. Paul further warns us concerning some people's self centred agenda rising out of the church: "Also from among yourselves men will rise up, speaking perverse things, to draw away the disciples after themselves." Acts 20:30. On of the perverse things spoken of in our time by false teachers is the false teaching on prosperity turning Mathew chapter 6:33 the other way round. Instead of teaching the church to focus on the things of God, they teach to focus on material things as they themselves amass great material wealth at the expense of the financially poor people in their congregations.

3. Religiosity versus Spirituality. With such doctrines taught in many churches, the level of living spiritual lives in Christ has diminished as religiosity has increased producing double standards and hypocrisy.

4. The church "club" and "business": This has not gone away yet as some leaders run the church as their personal money making business. They use all sorts of trickery, negative marketing techniques and totally non-biblical ways to extract money from unsuspecting congregation who fail to read the Bible and study for themselves. Jesus intend for us to prosper in all areas of our lives. Prosperity simply means lacking nothing in life according to Jesus. But now it

has been changed into money. "You will be rich because you are the son of the king" "sow a seed of "200 and I will pray for you for such and such anointing to come upon you..." are such lies been taught in many churches.

5. We still have problems living a holy life. We are still experiencing materialism, Envy, bitterness, sexual immorality, disunity and division, lack of love, looking down upon people, gossip, backbiting, rumours and many more. People come to church to be loved as Jesus did. On the contrary we do not show any friendliness but rather we seem to be as cold as ice and far as the stars!

6. Sin and Forgiveness. From the above issues identified in many churches, the preaching on sin and the good news on forgiveness seem to be a thing of the past as many preachers are so busy adding up other non biblical doctrines to make their sermons look 'powerful' and 'mysterious.' Well they have achieved that, as it is not from God.

We now know where our main focus should be and the tools the devil uses to distract us. Jesus has equipped us fully for the work of the ministry. We will now study on how to readjust and refocus our lives on God and Jesus in the next chapter.

It doesn't matter how far we have gone off track, Jesus is still ready to welcome us back. We are still the light of the world as Jesus said and we need to continue to look up to Jesus no matter how far we may be. Just as a ship on the dark sea, look up to the lighthouse and steer safely right up to it by focusing well.

-Chapter 3-

Refocusing on Jesus

"…..looking unto Jesus, the author and finisher of *our* faith.."Heb 12:1b

What causes blur vision?
In photography, one of the four listed causes of blurry photos is named as 'out of focus.' (Patterson). Although we have automatic digital cameras even on many smart phones, some images still become blurry when out of focus.

In real life situation, the same could be said of Adam and Eve when they lost focus on the word given to them to rule and have dominion over the earth. They rather chose to allow their selfish ambition of living as gods and becoming independent of God to rob them of all the power and authority given to them.

With this principle, the same could be said of our lives too. Those who do know Christ and have been living their lives outside Christ recommendation have also lost their focus on Him. For our theme, looking up to Jesus means focusing on Him at all times in our life. This means we could describe it as our spiritual life focus that also affects our physical life.

Lets now look out the outcome of focusing right or wrong as we used photography as our

Example. I believe this will throw some light on what we could do to adjust our focus.

The Outcome Of Focus.
Majority of the problems and many others identified could be as a result of where our focus is. Also indeed the heart of the human problem is the heart of human. What we decide to do contributes to the outcome due to the actions we take. I will share one example of how getting the right understanding and training could help us to readjust our focus on Christ for the best results.

Once again, in photography the outcome is said to be mainly the reflection of the level of focus. In my teen years in the 80's, my late dad had a "Yashica" camera (not too sure if the brand still exists). This was before the digital and automated focusing came. With that camera, you had to turn various knobs to get the correct focus on objects before you can get a good image. I am talking about knobs that controls ISO setting, Shutter speed, aperture and focus! Do you know what this is? Also not forgetting the 33mm film!

My sister and I used to borrow it on occasions. We took pictures with many either coming out as blurred or destroyed. Daddy taught us how to focus correctly and that resulted in better pictures.

Church' focus?
Our wrong focus reflects what is happening in our churches and in our lives. The good news

is that we have the opportunity to readjust or even completely refocus on Jesus.

That will put us back on track and go back to our first love. It would be a sad experience for Jesus to tell us that we lost our first love on the last day when it would be too late to repent and change our ways. We have the opportunity now. We don't want to be described by Jesus as the church, which was not hot or cold, or the one that think of being rich but were nothing.

> "...nevertheless, I have this against you, that you have left your first love," -Revelation 2:4

The warning in the book of revelation must be taken seriously. The change of focus will alter the situation that will spill over to impact our communities and the world. Revivals that have taken place right from the Old Testament times started with the people getting fed up of the status quo and taking the right action by refocusing on God.

People changed and that affected their communities. We can refocus on Jesus. It is good to know that Jesus has given us that opportunity.

Jesus said, "Remember therefore from where you have fallen; repent and do the first works, or else I will come to you quickly and remove your lampstand from its place-unless you repent."-Rev 2:5.

Trust based on credibility

It may seem very difficult to trust people in our time. Everyone seems to be suspicious of someone else. There is so much injustice and unfair treatment that even some Christians may not feel like trusting anyone. The betrayals and backbiting add to the pain and they are many instances.

We sometimes treat God in the same way maybe not intentional. We view God in the same way as our fathers (both biological and spiritual) in the way they treat us. If they treat us bad, that becomes our perception of God and vice versa. Let us refocus on who God is and the power He has given to His children. We must focus on Him through faith. We can do this by knowing and understanding who God is.

Understand Who God Is

God created the universe. This fact can be accepted by faith. God is faithful and will do whatever He says He will do. He is the author of all faithfulness and it is one of His attributes. He wants us to have faith in Him based on Who He is. He has never failed any of His children. If we can believe in this fact, then we should not fail to exercise our faith in times of trials. Hear are some of the pit stops;

1. The lack of knowledge of our rights as children of God robs us of many blessings and privileges. This is like Kings behaving and acting as servants. This can only result

when there is lack of knowledge and many are perishing because of it. Most importantly, it also robs us of knowing what our primary focus is as required from the Father and Jesus Christ.

2. Lack of wisdom and understanding of God's principle on faith. "If anybody lacks wisdom, let him ask of God, who gives to all liberally and without reproach, and it will be given to him."-James1: 5. The world cannot give us the wisdom of God. There is only one condition by which we can receive the wisdom of God as we read. There is a way to ask and a way to respond as taught by James:
"But let him ask in <u>faith,</u> with no doubting..." Jam 1:6a. Solomon asked God for wisdom to be able to rule over His people Israel. He had the right focus. God said because he did not ask for riches and the destruction of his enemies as a young man, He would give him wisdom and all the riches as well. That was powerful!!! The equivalent to this is in what Jesus taught us to do as we read in chapter one. "But seek first the Kingdom of God and His righteousness, and all these things shall be added to you." -Matthew 6:33.

3. Ignorance and giving up so easily without a 'fight.' "Fight the good fight of faith, and lay hold on eternal life…" -1Timothy 6:12a. There are some souls we need to 'snatch' from hell. We must not give up the good fight of faith. This is the only acceptable fight for us as children of God. We will study more on this.

Familiarity? Value
Familiarity can rob all from knowing exactly who our close associates are. We become so close to people or vice versa that we tend not to take time to get to know who they. This is very evident when no value it put on lives, talent and the gifts placed in them by God.

Remember, Judas walked with Jesus, the greatest God/Man on earth! It is likely he did not accept Jesus as His saviour. Although he was with Jesus there was something in his heart that was pulling him away from having a relationship with Him. He missed the greatest miracle of salvation and the Saviour. We will get to know how to avoid this.

Anything we put value on will benefit us depending on what type of value was put on. On the contrary anything we see or label as common will not work for us.

Jesus could not do so many miracles in His own hometown because of familiarity and the 'common' label put on Him.

They said of Him: "isn't this the son of Joseph, the carpenter..." What does a carpenter do? This attitude when not dealt with can slowly creep into any relationship and silently destroy it. We should not become so familiar with Jesus and forget Who He is. We should rather strive to get to know Him better.

God Keeps His Promises.

God keeps His promises because of Who He is. Have you made a promise and found it extremely difficult to keep due to some circumstances beyond your control? How many people have promised and failed you over these years? I have many who did. Do we sometimes see God as we see man? Men will promise and fail so we might think the same for God. On the contrary God is reliable and unlike man neither change nor fail.

> "God is not a man that He should lie,
> nor a son of man, that He should repent. Has He not said, and will He not do? Or has He spoken, and will He not make it good?"
> -Numbers 23.19

What an assurance to know that God does not operate as man. He will not ruin His reputation by going against His word.

God and Jesus Exist

How can we have a relationship with someone we think does not exist? When we start, continue, or renew our existing relationship with God, we should first <u>believe</u> and <u>know</u> that <u>God exists.</u> Knowing the existence of God is not an act of being foolish as many may think. It is the first step of the greatest relationship you can ever have in your life as it stretches into eternity.

Some reject the gospel of Jesus based on this. How can you believe in someone you do not see? How many of us see the pilot of the plane before take off? How many of us ask for the pilot's licence? This is also the first important foundation for relationship. You can only establish a relationship with something you have come to know.

By knowing that 'God is' (the Great I AM) we know Him as 'Elohim', that is God Almighty. In fellowship, He reveals Himself as Jehovah. In relationship with Jesus you get to know Him as the 'revealed Saviour,' one you can 'touch' and communicate with. You will not know Him as the world knows Him. That is the greatest privilege given to all.

1. Unchangeable God

Almighty God never changes. Jesus never changes. We identify Him as the Most High, Jehovah, and the Eternal One.

"Has thou not known? Has thou not heard, that the everlasting God, the Lord, the Creator of the end of the earth fainteth not, neither is weary." (Isaiah 40.28)-KJV

If God is all- powerful then why does it seem as though we are not experiencing His power and presence in these days? What has gone wrong? Has God forgotten our generation? The Bible has made it clear that God the father, Son and the Holy Spirit never change. God has now revealed Himself to us through His Son Jesus Christ. We now refer to God using Jesus Christ. "Jesus Christ the same yesterday and today and for ever" -Hebrew13.8

2. Jesus Christ (God) Always The Same
God has not changed in our time. Jesus has given us all the power and authority He has over the devil for His work. God said the "latter rain will be greater than the former."- He also said "I will pour out My Spirit upon all flesh" during the latter rain. We are indeed living in these end times or latter rain and should experience the greater anointing as promised by God Himself. These are the exciting times we are living in.

We may have some questions about what is happening in our time if we are suppose to have all this power and authority. How come we are not experiencing what the prophets of old did? How come Elijah and the great people of old made history worth recording in the Bible?

In trying to obtain some answers to these questions, we will look at the lives of some of the great men of old and how God mightily used them. At least that is what we may think. Have we ever thought along the lines of perhaps they may have allowed God to use them because of their obedience to and faith in Him. Let us look at the prophet Elijah and then Joshua in the next chapter as the results of focusing on God.

-Chapter 4-

Results of focusing on Jesus

"…..looking unto Jesus, the author and finisher of *our* faith.."Heb 12:1b

The Prophet Elijah.
This is the Biblical account concerning him: "Elijah was a man with a nature like ours, he <u>prayed earnestly</u> that it should not rain; and it did not rain on the land for three years and six months. And he <u>prayed again</u>, and the heaven gave rain and the earth produced its fruit."-James5: 17-18

How could he do that? The adjective "earnestly" portrays his level of faith. He was a man of great faith and one who knew God. Let us look at other unique things he did. In 1 king 1.18 Elijah is presented as a prophet of God who challenged Baal's prophet. The children of Israel at that time had forsaken God Almighty. Under the leadership of King Ahab and his wife Jezebel, they led the people of Israel to worship a false god called Baal.

Elijah threw a challenge to the prophets of Baal to a contest on mountain Carmel. The challenge was simple; the God who answers by fire will be God of Israel.

The prophets accepted this challenge and in attendance were the people of Israel.

Hundreds of Baal's prophets called on their god from morning until noon but nothing happened. Take note of this, "Elijah mocked them, and said, "cry aloud for he is a god, either he is talking, or he is pursuing, or he is in a journey, or peradventure he sleepeth and must be awaked" -1 King 18.27 (KJV). There was no answer from noon till evening. He could tease them because He knew Almighty God was alive.

Elijah built an altar of stones, prepared his bullock and dug a trench around it. The trench was filled with large volumes of water. The following was his prayer:

> "Lord God of Abraham, Jacob and Israel, let it be known this day that You are God in Israel and I am a servant and that I have done these things at your word. Hear me, O Lord, hear me, that this people may know that You are the Lord God, and You have turned their heart back again."-1 Kings 18:36b

Before one could blink fire came from heaven and consumed the sacrifice, the wood, the stones, dust and water in the trench. How did that happen? Why did God answer this man's request?

Answers:

1. God asked him to do something for Him and he did.

2. Elijah had faith in a faithful God's ability and trusted Him to do what He asked him to do. He had confident in God's word.
3. Elijah's total faith in God made these wonders happen.

Obedience, total faith and commitment- Elijah obeyed the Lord and was committed to carry out His task even to the point of risking his life. Can we do the same now? Can we challenge the evil happening in our communities? Haven't we been silent for too long? It is about time we break the culture of silence which is destroying our world and speak with the power of God to change evil situations.

Joshua.

Joshua asked God something very unusual. He was fighting against his enemies and the time came for the sun to set. He asked God to let the sun stand still so he could avenge his enemies, and GOD GRANTED HIM HIS REQUEST!!! God heard and obeyed a man's voice and even altered the normal course in His Own creation!

Who were these people that God did these mighty things through them? Were they very special than we are? As we read from James1.17-18 Elijah was just like any of us.

The difference is in their level of faith, trust and commitment to God through relationship and obedience. How far do you want to go with God?

Before Joshua was commissioned to take over from Moses, he was given some powerful instructions to follow. He was commanded never to let the book of the law depart from his lips but rather meditate on it day and night. And by so doing he would have prosperity and make his ways prosperous. He followed God's Word throughout his life and was prosperous. He trusted God and was obedient to Him.

He once challenged the whole nation of Israel to choose who they will serve as we read in the beginning of this book. He made it very clear to them that as for him and his family they will serve the Lord.

What We Have Studied So Far From These Examples?

1. We know that God never change. He is the same yesterday as He is today. He will be the same tomorrow so we can have this confidence.
2. Elijah and Joshua, together with all the great men God used were just like you and me.
3. God did not call some 'supermen' or 'superwomen.' They ate, drunk, became discouraged and fearful, and went through bad and good times, not forgetting

temptations and committing some serious sins.

God first call ordinary people with weaknesses like you and me, then empower them for kingdom service to affect the society and the world. The great men of old also disciplined themselves and remained faithful and determined to obey Him to the end. You can do likewise. Get your focus on Jesus right.

Jesus has Got All The Power And Authority
We read in Chapter one that Jesus has all the authority in heaven and earth and have given this to us, for His work. Let me explain this:

In this case to have authority means the power or right to give orders and make decisions or the right to rule. Authority and power combined are mighty weapons in the right hands. God has absolute authority and power as the creator of all things. This is same for Jesus, God the Son.

What Is Power?
Power is the force needed in implementing the right to rule, which is authority. The Greek word "*dunamis*", translated power is explained as the inherent power, which has the ability of reproducing itself as a dynamo.

Jesus, Who is the Word of God was recognised as one with authority when He taught in the synagogues.

This is true when the word of God is preached with the right focus and motive.

A classic example is found in the Bible when Jesus finished the redemptive work for mankind. His followers had the authority and power to cast out demons and to heal all diseases in Jesus name. The apostle Paul submitted to God's authority and went about doing the work of God, working miracles in the name of Jesus.

Angelic beings, both good and evil understand the principle of authority very well. Whoever is lower in rank respects those higher above them. There were seven sons of a Jewish priest named Sceva, who were not born again. These men attempted to cast out an evil spirit from a man in the name of Jesus "whom Paul preaches"

As these men were not born again as just read, the evil spirit recognized that they had no authority over him, so he taunted them by saying: "Jesus I know, and Paul I know; but who are you?" (Acts19.15) The evil spirit actually overpowered all seven and tore their clothes and chased them down the street. The possessed man also injured them. Now let us see the relationship between authority and power. Power is useless without the right authority. And remember Jesus gives all authority.

God's Power And Creation

God's power is recognised in all creation. This is evident in the creation of living beings. God put the power of reproduction in all living things.

Man has been given the power to reproduce after his kind in the God given set-up system through reproduction. This is both physical and spiritual when we become followers of Jesus. We need to "give birth" to many spiritual children because we have the power of reproducing after our kind.

Control
The Almighty God has set boundaries in all aspect of His creation. The moon and sun are positioned at where we see them never to be removed or changed unless God says so. He has given us the power to control and set standards in life. We can set these standards and practice them through discipline. These standards are in the Bible.

God gave Job an answer that gives us insight into His creation and also in charge of it. He said to Job:

"Tell Me, if you have understanding. Who determined the measurement? Surely you know it, or who stretched the line upon it. To what were its foundations fastened? Or who laid its cornerstone. When the stars sang together, and all the sons of God shouted for joy? Or who shut in the sea with doors, when its burst forth and issued from the womb. When I said, this far you may come, but no farther, and here your proud waves must stop. -Job38: 4-11

The Almighty God created the world and set boundaries for it including the seas and our moral lives. He fixed a limit to all things.

What an awesome controller!! It will only take God's control of affairs to keep the entire stars, sun, and moon suspended under God's firmament without any foundations. Remember the moon has never crashed into the sun ever since it was created!!!

We are now living in a permissive society whereby all absolutes are being removed. Do anything you want as far as it is all right with you. This is what is happening in society and destroying our world. This can no longer go on as we have the power to set limits to help rescue our ailing society without any moral limits.

The Power Of Submission

We cannot study the subject on power and authority in the context of faith without touching on submission. Jesus described the act of submission as "great faith". He was invited into the house of a centurion to heal one of his sick servants. Before He got to the house the centurion came out and said:

> "Lord, do not trouble Yourself, for I am not worthy that You should enter under my roof. Therefore I did not even think of myself worthy to come to You. But say the word and my servant will be healed." –Luke 7:6.

This was his reason for this act of faith: "For I am a man placed under authority having soldiers under me. And I say to one 'Go' and he goes; and to another 'come,' and he comes.... -Luke 7:8.

Jesus marveled at him on hearing this and said to those standing around: "I say to you, I have not found such great faith, not even in Israel". -Luke 7:9.

The principle of submission is very crucial. I describe submission as backing or taking our hands or self off what rightfully belongs to Jesus and God. Submitting to Jesus' is an act of great faith. This man had absolute faith in Jesus' authority and ability. We do not need to see the answer before stepping out in faith. Whatever Jesus has said He will do. You receive His authority as you voluntarily lay yours down. It is an act of faith built on obedience and love.

In the story of Abraham and Isaac, it sounded as though God was undermining His own purpose and plan. Isaac was the son of promise and miracle from Him. Abraham's faith had grown over the years as he had consistent relationship with God.

Although he might have been shocked by God's request to sacrifice Isaac by killing him, he submitted to Him. He said, "God will provide for Himself the lamb for the burnt offering"-Genesis 22:8. Abraham took his hands off what belonged to God and in so doing passed the test of faith. The result was the blessings that we who have accepted God's free gift of eternal life are also enjoying today.

In Submitting to Jesus we will be lifted up. God resist the proud but lifts up the humble. Submission is in humility to God. Humility is not humiliation as some may have interpreted. Submit to God daily and see your confidence in Him helping us to survive any faith test.

We can be reassured that God has the ultimate power and that will never run or dry out and we can rely on Him to do whatever is required of us to fulfill His purpose for us and out world.

-Chapter 5-

Focus On Relationship.

".....looking unto Jesus, the author and finisher of *our* faith.."Heb 12:1b

Building Relationship Through Faith.
A study through the Bible reveals that the great men of old had one thing in common. They pleased God. In their walk with God they sought after Him diligently, and continued to have, develop and maintain an intimate relationship with Him. This was based on faith. This fits the description of focus.

This type of relationship with God does not happen overnight. It is a long journey, which requires dedication, trust, and commitment. We also need to have the desire to do it or it becomes burdensome. The good news is that it is possible.

The bottom line is this; they all had unwavering faith in a faithful God, and paid the price for it together with the rewards. Why is it so important to please God? This is what the Bible says:

"But without faith it is impossible to please God, for he who comes to God must believe that He is and that He is a rewarder of those who diligently seek Him."- Hebrews11.6

This powerful verse is the basis for intimate relationship with God in order to connect to Him.

To be empowered means we need to be connected to the source of power to ignite our generation. Let us walk by faith and trust in His word. It is impossible for us to please God without faith. On the contrary it is possible to please God with faith. Faith is recognised when we act on it. It is only seen in its works.

Faith– required Factor
We have studied that without faith we cannot please God in any way. What is faith that makes it so important?

> "Now faith is the substance of things hoped for, the evidence of things not seen.-Heb11: 1

This is one of the best if not the best definition of faith given in the Bible. My definitions of faith are based on my understanding on how I have lived it during these years. Faith is the bridge between the promised word of God and the physical manifestation of that promise.

Faith is bringing the future into the present. It is the expectation to receiving something from the supernatural and using hope as an anchor to hold on until it materialises.

Hope is the anchor that never fails, but aid in the faith process. Holding on till the end will produce the result of the promise. Although faith is spiritual, the results are seen in the physical as well.

Whenever I witness to people, it is evident that one of the main reasons they reject Jesus Christ is based on the concept on faith. The argument is the same. How can you have faith in someone you cannot see? The answer is the same as the one read earlier.

Jesus said, "That which is born of the flesh is flesh, and that which is born of the Spirit is Spirit." It could be almost impossible to interpret spiritual things with physical knowledge. Many have experienced this as well during evangelism or sharing the good news of the gospel of Jesus Christ.

How can you believe in someone or something, which is not necessarily substantiated by proof, especially scientific proof as many try to hide behind it? If this is the issue let us consider some few things we do without considering the consequences. I sited the first example earlier on with the pilot.

Investment – Expectation Of High Returns?
Millions around the world are investing so much of their lives in various things. Some are investing for their children's future in education. Some invest in deposits, corporate bonds, stock market, works of art and many other funds. It is good to plan for the future. On the other hand these are not guaranteed and have some degree of risk as told by our financial investment experts. The children who you invest so much for may even decide to drop out of school.

Why all this investments? Everyone has invested in something in one way or the other. One of the reasons for any investment is simply to receive a high return on it or some benefit of some sort. This could be in the form of profits, better-educated children with good job prospects, and all sorts of high expectation. No businessperson goes into a contract with the expectation to loose.

We have faith in these temporal things that are not stable and subject to change without any warning, not considering who may be affected or not. Kingdoms do rise and others have and will fall, civilizations will keep changing, culture and lifestyles will continue changing. Companies and organisations will continue to fall and new ones established. Life will keep changing daily whether we like it or not. Everything within "time" is subject to change. Just look at yourself, and compare your current picture to that taken last ten years. Any changes?

You could wake up one morning to realise that the investment bank you trusted with your life savings has collapsed. In 2008, our world experienced one of the worst financial crises in history and it took many years afterwards for recovery. Technology is constantly changing quicker than anything imaginable. Everything will keep changing except the word of God and God Himself! Things of eternal value never change in time. Let us get our focus right on such things.

Observations:

1. In London and some other countries, people queue up at banks at the end of the financial year to have their interest added to their accounts or investments.
2. The loyalties that keep people in these investment institutions are sometimes rewarded.
3. We have faith in these institutions.
4. We trust in these institutions for higher returns at the end of the investment period. When these expectations are not met some people may sometimes complain bitterly.

If it is okay to take the risk in chasing after things that seem volatile and not guaranteed, then I believe you will agree that it is okay to seek God and His kingdom, which we can find and have the guaranteed assurance of His love and purpose fulfilled in our lives.

The Bible warns us not to lay up treasures on earth where moth and rust destroy and where thieves break in and steal; "but lay up for yourselves treasures in heaven, where neither moth nor rust destroys and where thieves do not break in and steal." -Matthew 6.19-20.

God does not want us to seek only after temporal things, but He wants us not to forget the permanent ones as well.

God want us to set our priorities right by saying

"For where your treasure is, there your heart will be also" -Matthew 6.21.

It is not wrong to have material things. It is Jesus who gives us all good things. On the other hand our priority must be right.

If an experienced professional hacker can get into the most secured computer sites such as the military or government in the world and others are able to bomb some secured facilities as well, then it could be true that nothing is secured in this life except the Word of God.

Seek God Diligently
We cannot call ourselves into the family of God. The good news is that God has provided a way for this to be achieved by giving us an open invitation through the accepting of Jesus Christ as our Saviour. The reason why faith is so important is the fact that the God Who has called us is Himself faithful. "He who calls you is faithful, Who also will do it."-1Thes 5.24. Works always accompanies faith.

God is faithful because He will do whatever He says concerning your life. What does it mean to seek God diligently? This is simply looking earnestly for Him until you find Him. How do you find Him? God is found in His word. He was revealed through the Lord Jesus in His given word, the Bible. He is not far as we may think.

When we diligently seek God through faith, you hold the devil in the corner or arena of faith.

On the other hand the devil's ultimate desire is to hold you in the arena of fear, which has torment. Fear has the capability to sow the seed of hopelessness in us. It can torment and frustrate us until we loose our focus on Jesus and begin to accept all forms of negative things. It can cause you to loose your self worth as well. With faith in God, you defeat Satan daily by frustrating his plans against you. You confess and act on what Jesus says about you.

Seeking to know Jesus Christ comes with a price tag as well as great rewards. The lower the price to pay, the lower the reward, and vice versa. Seeking God diligently means having the ultimate desire to fellowship with Him daily. This comes with total commitment to reading and studying the Bible and choosing to do what Jesus says. Talk to Jesus every time, as you will do to your family or friends hopefully. This is when our will and desires are surrendered to Him. This is how to get to know Him and continually build a strong and intimate relationship as well.

Athletes and sport personalities train very hard consistently and deny themselves of many things in order to achieve their number one goal. They go to the extreme in order to achieve this. This goal is simply to win the gold, which will be competed with many others who also aim for the same reward.

In the same way our consistency in seeking after God through relationship and fellowship will determine how close we will get to Him. In this case, communication will help with the development of the relationship. It will bring us closer and closer to Jesus.

Friends, the diligent walk with Jesus is not like the 'raincoat' attitude. This is when we pray to Him when things go wrong and we have done all we could possibly do and failed as humans. We normally term this situation as "beyond human control".

Even at this stage, it is still alright to seek Him in such times if you have never had the opportunity to hear the gospel. But it is best to know Jesus as a friend and saviour. No friend of ours will like to have a 'raincoat' type of relationship whereby they only take from you and never add anything to your life- From the biology I studied many years ago, that may be described as a 'parasitic' attitude.

Relationship should be a daily routine and the communication process improved. Remember, the more people or relationships stick together through communication, the more they get to know each other and become more intimate.

Jesus has already given us the key to build relationship with Him. In Matthew 7:7 Jesus taught by saying "ask and it will be given; seek and you will find; knock, and it will be opened to you". When you ask God for His presence and power, He will give exactly what you asked. Ask the Holy Spirit of God to be your friend and see what happens. Seek God diligently and you will surely find Him. Can we really seek God diligently? Yes I did, so can you.

Can we really do this as Abraham and

Moses? Can we become the friends of God? The answer is yes. You too can become a friend of Jesus depending on how far you want to go and how much price you are willing to pay. God even see His children as heirs and joint heirs with His only begotten Son Jesus Christ, better than friends. The road may not be smooth but the desire to do it with the help of the Holy Spirit will see you through. Jesus calls us His friends and brethren.

Remember the people in the Old Testament did not have the presence of the Holy Spirit as we have Him today. We are more privileged. The problem is that, many people may see or think of following Jesus as some kind of a "joy killer". They believe strongly that God does not want them to have 'fun.' This depends on how fun is defined. This is totally false, as God want us to have joy and peace more abundantly in the right way, which will not destroy us in any way, be it in the spiritual or natural sense.

The apostle Peter asked a question which helps to answer this. He asked Jesus: "see we have left all and followed You." Here was Jesus' answer, which is a great promise to us.

> "Assuredly, I say to you, there is no one who has left house or brothers or sisters or father or mother or wife or children or lands, for My sake and the gospels, <u>who</u> shall not receive a hundredfold now in this time- houses and brothers and sisters and mothers and children and lands, with persecutions- and in the age to come,

eternal life."-Mark 10:28-30

All these blessings are guaranteed with trials as well. We will study on how to deal with the trials as we continue to our study.

Attention Seekers.
There are many people and things seeking our attention. Majority of these may be engineered to distract us from our relationship with Christ. These include some adverts from the media, television programmes and many others. All these are attracting our attention and our loyalty. It has been said that millions are watching television at an alarming rate. Can you imagine if we spend part of these times reading about Jesus, praying and practicing His life? Our faith will increase and our desire to win souls will soar!!

Unfortunately, many followers of Christ have been caught in this web. Some are finding it very hard to be fully committed to the things of God. What surprises me is how people can watch television programmes (movies) for hours and struggle to pray for ten minutes, not forgetting the reading of 400 page novels but finds it difficult to read few versus in scripture.

One of the solutions to this is to set and get our priorities right. I cannot over emphasise on this. We need to change our attitude and mindset. This is God's ultimate solution to how we tackle this as we read at the beginning of this study from chapter one: "but seek **first** the **kingdom of God** and His righteousness, and all these things shall be added to you. "Therefore do not worry about tomorrow for tomorrow will worry about its own things". -Matthew 6.33-34

This is His promise: Have a wonderful relationship with Me and receive all your hearts desire within His will. We need to read the Bible as that is the only way to know Who Jesus is and what He has said about us. All of His promises are yes and in Him amen. Keep this scripture in mind and never forget it:

> "Being confident of this very thing, that He Who has begun a good work in you will complete it until the day of Jesus Christ." - Philippians 1.6.

Finally we should be aware of Jesus' willingness to have a relationship with us. He is still saying to you "behold I stand at the door and knock, if anyone hears My voice and opens the door, I will come in to him and dine with him and him with Me. -Revelation 3.20

This invitation is open to all. This is what the renowned people of old like Abraham and Elijah accepted and were able to do what we read about. They opened the door of their heart and allowed God to be the centre of their lives. His presence brought His power that made them what they were. Do you want what they had? Remember the door is open to all, and no one is above the other. You have the same opportunity as they did so open your heart to Jesus.

We have studied on how to build relationship with Jesus by faith. In the next chapter we will be given the key to this process.

-Chapter 6-

The Faith Journey

.....looking unto Jesus, the author and finisher of *our* faith.."Heb 12:1b

The Miracle Of Seed-Faith.
As we now know the importance of faith when it come to our relationship with God Almighty and Jesus, I believe it will be a good starting point to explore what Jesus taught concerning this,

Jesus teaching on faith used the sower and the seed in a parable to explain the kingdom of heaven. In this parable the seeds fell on various types of soils. When the disciples asked about what it meant, Jesus explained that the seed is the word of God. (Please read and study Matthew 13:1-23)

In the gospel of John, Jesus is revealed as the Word made flesh. Now from these studies we can see that Jesus is the Word of God, which is the seed. Faith comes by hearing the word of God. Faith comes when we hear the words of Jesus. "So then faith comes by hearing, and hearing by the word of God. -Romans 10:17. As a seed, Faith has the full life of Jesus. This life has the potential to grow.

Jesus taught on faith using the mustard seed to explain a very crucial point. The only reason He used so many parables involving earthly things was to explain spiritual kingdom truths for our own understanding and benefit. He said:

"The kingdom of heaven is like a mustard seed which a man took and sowed in his field, which is the least of all the seeds, but when it is grown it is greater than the herbs and becomes a tree, so that the birds of the air come and nest in it's branches."
-Matthew 13:32.

According to Sproule (1980), botanically the mustard seed is not the smallest seed. However, he suggests that if Jesus was talking about the seed known to the people compared to that of the whole earth then that statement was right for the context and audience.

What was Jesus trying to teach us in the Matthew 13:32? Why did He liken faith in God to a seed and not a horse or an eagle? The mustard seed is known to be physically small in size compared to others. This tiny seed when planted in the soil grows to be a great tree!! This is a divine miracle and not logic!! In comparing faith in God to a small seed, Jesus was teaching us that faith has the potential and ability to grow without limit. Knowing more about Jesus will cause our faith to increase daily.

The journey of our faith in God starts with looking up onto Jesus, Who is the **Author** and **finisher** of our faith. -Hebrews 12:2a, which is our theme scripture for this study. He is the focus of our faith. Other Bible translates this as the "perfecter of our faith". Within time there is always a start and finish. Every creation has an author. Rolex watches, Mercedes Benz and all products have authors or originators. Let us look up to Jesus to build our faith.

a. Start the faith journey with small strides. It is okay to start small.

b. When this seed is sown in your spirit (heart), it has the potential to grow. This growth continues with your relationship with Jesus by reading and acting on the word from the Bible.

c. Your faith (as a seed) when watered, and under favourable conditions can grow to be great, just as Abraham, Elijah, Moses and the others. Read the Bible daily.

d. Your great faith should benefit many who come your way. Your words of encouragement should give life to those who have lost the desire to live. You can help many with your variety of wealth by giving them the basic needs in life, which would be the work of your faith. Faith without works is dead.

Conditions For Growth Of Seed-Faith.

For a seed to grow successfully, conditions should be good and favourable. For example, some seed will survive in soil with much water while others will die in the same condition. The important factor here is to make sure the seed geminate and grow very well in the right type of environment. The seed must be taken care of from the day it is planted until it bears fruit.

In the same way seed – faith need to grow and keep growing. There is no limit to the growth of our faith until we see Jesus. On that day, the Bible declares that faith and hope will not be needed any longer but love will continue forever. Faith and hope will become reality. You will no longer have faith in Jesus because we will see Him in person. Until then we still need faith to live the Christian life to impact our world at the same time fulfilling our God given destinies.

The best way to know Jesus through fellowship is to ask the Holy Spirit to come into your life and be your friend and guide. There is no formula as A* B=AB, but purely on the basis of personal relationship. When this happens, the Holy Spirit Who inspired chosen people to write the Bible will reveal who Jesus and the Father are to you. You can then have revelation knowledge of who Jesus is. This will not come through any theological college but through personal relationship with Him.

It is amazing to know how children can recite the words in a television advert. How can they do that? The more they hear it the more it sticks in their memory. In the same manner the best way to keep our faith growing is to keep hearing and continue to hear God's word, over and over...until Jesus Christ become "flesh" to us. "So then faith comes by hearing and hearing by the word of God" -Romans 10.17.

Let us consider these favourable and unfavourable conditions that affect our ability to have faith in God. There are two main factors involved I believe could be named as 'belief' and 'doubt.'

1. 'Belief' (in God's word) should undoubtedly go a long a way to help to build up our faith. It is a faith activator and motivator. It also strengthens us in the Lord concerning His word.

2. On the other hand 'doubt' could be described as a complete faith killer. Satan opposes God in every way. When God says to you "you can make it in life," Satan will say the opposite "you can never make it." James gave an account comparing faith to doubt as follows: " But let him ask in faith, with no doubting, for he who doubts is like a wave of the sea driven and tossed by the wind. For let not that man suppose that he will receive anything from the Lord; he is a double-minded man, unstable in all his ways."-James 1:6-8

This is how serious this issue is. We cannot belief and doubt at the same time. Jesus Christ on His earthly assignment went to many places working miracles and doing great wonders. The workings of His miracles were restricted in some areas where the environment of faith and belief were not present.

On the contrary, miracles were numerous in places where the people demonstrated faith. Remember what we studied earlier. The atmosphere of belief creates the faith environment for the power of God to move mightily.

Doing what Jesus did?
There was a time when Jesus took Peter, James and John to a high mountain.

Over there He was transfigured before their eyes. (Please Read Matthew 17.1-11). After this wonderful experience, they came down from the mountain and were met by a great multitude. Immediately a man came forward to Jesus and kneeling down before Him said "Lord have mercy on my son, for he is an epileptic and suffers severely, for he often falls into the fire and often into the water, so I brought him to Your disciples but they could not cure him."-Matthew 17:15-16

1. As a follower of Christ, the world may secretly expect you to be able to do what Jesus did.
2. They will become disappointed when we fail to live up to that expectation.

Can we really do what Jesus did? Let us look at Jesus' response. "Oh faithless and perverse generation, how long shall I be with you? How long shall I bear with you? Bring him here to Me - Matthew 17.17

a. Jesus was so disappointed in them the same way He will be with us if we fail Him in the area of faith. He was expecting just a little faith and some corresponding action as they have heard Him teach and see Him do miracles.
b. In fact God becomes weary of us when we appear before him faithless. Nothing will ever happen with a heart full of unbelief.

Jesus rebuked the demon and it came out. The child was cured from that very hour.

The disciples later went to Jesus privately and asked Him why they were not able to cure the boy. Jesus' answer was so simple and the same, "because of your unbelief; assuredly, I say to you, if you have faith as a mustard seed, you will say to this mountain, move from here to there and it will move; and nothing will be impossible for you.
-Matthew 17.20.

We can see that the subject on faith compared to a mustard seed was used to encourage us to have at least a bit of it. A little faith is one hundred per cent better than none at all which amounts to unbelief. The disciples failed simply because of unbelief!

Remember input equals output and do not forget that it works equally on God's principle on seedtime and harvest time. The best condition for our faith to grow is 'belief.'

There is a great lesson in the story we read. The father of the child described what happens when the demon possessed him. "And often he has thrown him both into the fire and into the water to destroy him. But if You can do anything, have compassion on us and help us." -Mark 9:22. That sounds like Satan at work!! He likes to do the same to children, our friends, business and us. Jesus exposed his works and operation as this:

The thief does not come except to steal, and to kill, and to destroy. I have come that they may have life, and that they may have *it* more abundantly.- John 10:10. We can stop top him.

Jesus recognised disbelief and helped him. "If you can believe, all things are possible to him who believes."- Mk 9:23. It is a choice to believe or disbelief, but both come with consequences. Immediately the man responded, "Lord I believe, help my unbelief!"(verse 24). When we are drawn into disbelief in any situation remember to ask the Lord for help!!

-Chapter 7-

God's Awesome Presence

.....looking unto Jesus, the author and finisher of *our* faith.."Heb 12:1b

God's power and His Presence.
This is the secret key to a successful Christian walk with God in faith. We will look at two examples in the Old Testament. An encounter with Jesus means His presence. The presence of Jesus comes with all His attributes and power as well and that cannot be detached.

1. **Moses:** God called Moses and directed him to lead His children, the people of Israel from the land of bondage into His promised land. On the way to the Promised Land, the people disobeyed God on so many occasions even after seeing His numerous miracles and wonders. One of such disobedience attracted God's anger. All along the presence of God and His hand led them with divine protection day and night. The demonstration of His power, which came through His presence, was literally seen by all the people.

After their disobedience God promised to send an angel to lead them instead of Himself.

The reason was that His anger could consume them on the way. God hated and still hate idolatry and murmurings, which are the products of lack of faith and trust in Him. What was Moses' response to God's change of plan? What would you have done in this situation?

Moses said to God, "If Your Presence does not go with us, do not bring us up from here. -Ex 33:15. In other words if Your presence will not go with me, then I am not going anywhere. So the Lord spoke to Moses face to face as a man speaks to a friend. -Exodus 33:11. Moses continued to communicate with God until He said, "My presence will go with you".

What an encounter!! Why did Moses intercede on behalf of the people of Israel? Moses understood what it meant to have fellowship with God. He knew that the power of God for deliverance, salvation and promotion only came with His presence. This is the ultimate secret. You can't experience God's power without His presence. You cannot experience His presence without fellowship through faith in Christ.

2. God delivered Israel into the hands of their enemies for forty years due to their disobedience. These enemies were the Philistines.

God made provision for deliverance once again. He sent an angel to announce the birth of Sampson. Some specific instructions were given concerning him and God's presence over his life. God said no razor should touch his head as he was to be separated for God's work.

> "And the Spirit of the Lord began to move upon him at Mahaneh Dan...." -Judges: 13.25.

Sampson's strength came as the Spirit of God moved upon him. He killed a lion with his bare hands, caught three hundred foxes and freed himself from being tied with new ropes. "Then the Spirit of the Lord came mightily upon him and the ropes that were on his arms became like flax that is burned with fire and his hands broke loose..." - Judges 15:14. He also killed one thousand enemies with only a jawbone of a donkey.

Sampson's disobedience in disclosing the secret of his strength saw the departure of God's presence from him. The presence of God departed with the power, which gave him the strength. Remember when the Holy Spirit leaves a believer's life it is not announced until you try to do the same things that involves Him. In Sampson's case when he woke up after the disclosure of his secret through having a relationship with the wrong choice of woman, he realised that the strength of God has left.

> "Finally, Sampson told her his secret, 'my hair has never been cut' he confessed, for I am dedicated to God... if my head were shaved, my strength would leave me, and I would become as weak as anyone else'...

Delilah realised he had finally told her the truth, so she sent for the Philistine leaders.... Delilah lulled Sampson to sleep with his head in her lap and she called a man to shave off his hair. Then she cried out "Sampson! The philistines have come to capture you! When he woke up, he thought, "I will do as before and shake myself free." But he didn't realise the Lord had left him. (Extracts from Judges: 16.17-20 NLT).

He was taken as a prisoner and put into prison. In prison no one realised his hair was growing. One day he prayed to God to remember him one more time and strengthen him. He wanted to take vengeance on his captors who removed his eyes. The people he killed on the day of his death were more than those during his lifetime.

The vital issue here is the presence of God and His power that comes with it. The power we need in this life belongs to Him. We need God's power to help us build our strong faith to live a holy life in this adulterous and perverse generation. Let us do our best to value our faith in God by obeying His commands.

On the contrary, even if you find yourself in Sampson's situation, God always give a second chance. All you need to do is to come back to Him through faith and repentance. He will restore you and continue fellowship with you. Never start a day without the presence of God. Much will be achieved within a short time with His presence.

In the early church days, the apostles did so many miracles because the Lord Jesus Christ was with them. He was not with them physically, but God's presence need not be physical. When His presence comes, you will definitely know because God the Holy Spirit will speak and give directions and instructions.

Faith Draws God's Power.
During the earthly ministry of Jesus Christ, He showed us some examples to follow. The Messiah was working so many miracles and mighty wonders. This brought about His fame spreading through cities like wild fire in a dry forest. Some of the following true experiences from the Bible will help us apply our faith in this walk with Christ.

1. Many people gathered in a town called Capernaum when they heard of Jesus' arrival. Mark 2:3 gives an account of a paralytic man carried by four men who could not come near to where Jesus was because of the large crowd. These guys decided to do whatever it took to get the sick man to Jesus. They went to the roof of the house Jesus was ministering, removed part of it and lowered the bed of the sick man at the place where He was.

"When Jesus **saw their faith,** He said to the paralytic, 'son your sins are forgiven you, I say to you arise take up your bed and go to your house. - Mark 2:5, 11.

What can we learn from this? Faith in Jesus Christ will move us into action. "Thus also faith by itself, if it does not have works is dead. But do you want to know O foolish man, that faith without works is dead? –James 2:17, 20. This was addressed to those who think having faith or works alone is enough. It is required of us to have both.

It only takes our faith in God and our response, which is the action or works to draw His power for our life. The Bible said Jesus saw their faith and that kind has the ability to draw the power of God for the healing of the paralysed man.

Like this sick man, your situation may have 'paralysed' you; health wise, finance etc. but remember your faith in Jesus' ability will see you through. Jesus did not see their muscles or the hopelessness of the situation, but saw faith. **When God sees faith He is compelled to respond in the same way He respond to salvation for all.**

Faith Is Rewarded.
Let see the works, which accompanied their faith:

    a. The paralytic man and the other four heard about Jesus and all He did, the blind saw, the lame walked and the dead were raised back to life. Their faith was built up.

    b. They determined or drew a plan of action to get this paralysed man to

Jesus no matter the cost or obstacles in their way.
c. They took practical steps to implement their plan, which worked.
d. Their faith was rewarded!!! Faith in Jesus will always be rewarded!

Remember God is obliged to act whenever He sees faith exercised in accordance with His Word and will.

2. Once Jesus and His disciples entered a city called Jericho. When they came out of it a great multitude met them as usual. A blind man by name Bartimaeus sat by the road and begged for alms. Jesus went along the road where this blind man sat one day and this was what happened. When he heard of Jesus, he shouted aloud "Jesus, Son of David, have mercy on me." –Mk 10:47

Many people shunned his company and shouted at him to keep quite. Could you imagine this scenario? The more they 'shut him up' the more he cried out aloud "Jesus, Son of David, have mercy on me."

Immediately, Jesus stopped and asked him to be called. The same people who asked him to keep quite called him to Jesus.

"So Jesus answered and said to him 'what do you want Me to do for you? The blind man said to Him, "Rabboni, that I may receive my sight.

Then Jesus said to him "go your way: **your faith** has made you well. And immediately he received his sight and followed Jesus on the road. -Mark 10:47-49.

Why did Jesus ask him this question? Jesus already knew what he wanted. However, He wanted to see faith in action. Out of the abundant of the heart the mouth speaks. When faith abounds in our heart we confess it. What moved him to go to Jesus?

   a. The blind man heard about Jesus and what He had been doing. He may have heard the wonders and miracles He was doing. Faith comes by hearing, and hearing the word of God as we read in previous chapters.
   b. He seized the opportunity of his lifetime when it came his way and exercised his faith by determining to attract Jesus' attention. He made up his mind to believe in Him and to achieve his goal without anything getting in his way.
   c. The power in his faith touched the healing power in Jesus, which attracted His attention. When Jesus asked the blind man what he wanted, he knew exactly what he wanted.
   d. Once again his faith was rewarded!!

There are countless examples, which can help us with our faith in Christ. We will look at two more interesting examples.

3. On another occasion Jesus had crossed over to the other side and as usual a great multitude gathered to Him. One of the rulers of the Jewish synagogue by name Jarius came and asked Jesus for a favour. He said "my little daughter lies at the point of death, come and lay your hand on her that she may be healed."-Mark 5:22-23

When Jesus was on His way to Jarius house, something dramatic happened which is worth studying. There was a lady who suffered from what the Bible described as 'flow of blood'. The Bible said she had suffered many things from physicians for twelve years! Does this sound familiar? Have you gone through similar experiences? Get your faith up, something is about to happen just as it did to this lady. (Story in Mark 5:24-34)

   a. Medical science couldn't help her. This lady had spent all that she had, but did not get better, rather worse.
   b. When she heard about Jesus, she determined to come close and touch the tip of His garment regardless of whoever was around Him.

What drove her to do that? She knew her label as a public disgrace because of her infirmity. It was her faith in Jesus' ability that motivated her to take that bold step. She came behind Jesus and touched His garment.

That was all she wanted compared to the Jewish leader who wanted Jesus to travel to His house and lay lands on his daughter. This could prove that there are various levels of faith.

Immediately this lady executed her plan of faith, the fountain of blood dried up and she felt in her body that she was healed of her affliction. What a wonderful experience she had!! Did her faith draw God's power? Yes it did! This can happen to you even as you read now. Let your faith draw Jesus' power to help you.

The people around Jesus pushing and touching Him had no effect on His power until He said, "Who touched my clothes"? Jesus asked because "immediately He knew in Himself that power had gone out of Him." His own disciples got a bit confused when Jesus asked, "who touched Me?" They said to Him "many are touching and thronging you and you ask this question".

The woman came forward and told Jesus the whole story. Jesus said, "daughter your faith had made you well, go in peace and be healed of your affliction."(Mark 5.34). Ordinary touch has no effect on Jesus' power, but the touch of faith draws His power.

This experience is true. We draw God's power when our faith is released. The greater the release of your faith, the greater His power is drawn.

This involves intimate relationship and the ultimate trust in Jesus' ability.

Remember, your faith will draw Jesus' power to solve unthinkable problems and issues of life. Faith is like a magnet that attracts Jesus' power; so let yours become bigger than any problem you face in this life. Jesus is Lord of all.

The Power Of Faith.

Jesus and His disciples came out of a town called Bethany and were hungry. He saw a fig tree afar off, which had, leaves on it. Jesus went closer to see if he could find some fruit on it to eat. To His disappointment there was none on it, for it was not the season for figs. Jesus cursed the tree and said,

> "Let no one eat from you ever again" and His disciples heard it. The following morning as they passed by they saw that the fig tree had dried up from the roots. Peter remembering brought it to Jesus attention. "The fig tree which you cursed has withered away. Jesus said: HAVE FAITH IN GOD.
>
> "For assuredly, I say to you, whosoever says to this mountain, 'be removed and be cast into the sea, and does not doubt in his heart, but believes that those things he says will be done, he will have whatever he says."-Mark11.22-23

Application of our faith in whatever we say or do, whether in the form of conversation or prayer will have strong effect on the outcome. Jesus once again used the removal of mountains to illustrate the power of having faith in God's ability. Nothing can stand in the way of faith in action. It will remove or level any obstacle in its way.

Never let doubt rob you of your miracle. When you speak forth believe that those things you say will surely come to pass within God's will. All things are real and created by God, both the visible and invisible, He is the One in charge.

Now there is something deeper and amazing that will change your prayer life. Jesus sad "therefore I say to you, <u>whatever thing</u> you <u>ask</u>, when you <u>pray,</u> <u>believe</u> that you <u>receive</u> and <u>you will have them</u>." -Mark11.24

1. God has made it clear in His word that you can ask for anything in faith. This means that we ask for things according to the will of God without any exceptions.
2. Apply the definition of faith. Believe that you will receive the things you have prayed for. Start to see the substance and evidence of whatever was asked for as though they are tangible. Faith will convert them from invisible into visible. Hang on to faith till the end.
3. Divine law of faith applies. When we ask from our physical point of view, we need to move into the

supernatural to establish it in the realms of the spirit. The answer is then released in the physical realm if what we asked is in that realm.

Take note of what Jesus said, "Whatever thing". Do not limit God or try to help Him in any way. God doesn't need your help. He is sovereign and He will do what He purpose to do.

I have seen and continue to experience the hand of God on my life. He has been working so many miracles in my life through healing me from diseases and protection from car crashes and the likes. I started my Christian journey based on faith due to the circumstances at the time of my coming to accept Jesus and His calling to preach and teach.

Relentless faith in a faithful Saviour has kept me all these years. God is still in the business of working miracles so release your faith through belief and experience the impossible too in all areas of your life.

-Chapter 8-

How To Impact your World.

.....looking unto Jesus, the author and finisher of *our* faith.."Heb 12:1b

The People Who Can Make A Difference.
You don't need to go far to know that our world is in trouble. It is all over in our tabloids and news. We have drug addiction and trafficking problems, murder, rape and all sorts of evil acts. We are living in a time which one will kill another for their gold watch. No value is placed on lives anymore. We may have either experienced crime directly or indirectly. When this happens to our friends and loved ones we somehow share in their pain.

We have a more serious problem whereby Satan is being portrayed as 'good'. Satan is no longer hiding his identity. It is now on television and many are wearing 'T' shirts displaying 'hell' and "Satan's property". People are now identifying themselves with Satan. This is the kind of world we are living in today.

Is this the kind of world we will like to live in? What will happen in the next ten years? What kind of world do we want our children to live in? How will it look like in the next twenty years?

Whatever decision we make today will affect what will happen in the future. We can make that difference like Elijah, Jesus and the apostles.

Any Solutions? We need the right solution for the right problem. Spiritual issues must be dealt with spiritually. When we are hungry for food, drinking of water might be a possible solution but eating proper food is the right solution.

Many people are relying on governments and other sources for solutions to society's problems. The sad news is that we are all aware of the failures on their side. Many a time governments and leaders make wrong decisions.

One typical example happened in the United Kingdom. Public houses selling alcohol to the public used to close between 11pm to 12midnight. The medical association expressed concern about the excessive consumption of alcohol and its deadly effects on people's health. In response to this, the parliament and the government licensed the public houses to open 24hours. Great solution??

The prisons are also housing about thousands of inmates. In finding a solution to this the government proposed to build new prisons. You would have thought the pubs would be shut to try and cut down on the problem identified in the first example.

Secondly you would have thought that the root cause of evil acts would be investigated.

Satan is hiding behinds these acts and he is not even mentioned. We are the ones who can make a change. We are the light of the world. Let us look at some practical steps to get ready to change our world.

Preparing For The Change.
We now know Who to focus on. We have learnt where our priority should be. Jesus has given us the power and authority to rule and have dominion over every situation on earth. The lifestyles of great men of faith are examples to us to emulate to change our world. Now we need to equip ourselves with the knowledge of the word of God. This begins with examining ourselves by first switching allegiance. We are either totally for Christ or none for Him.

The first step is always to be born again by the spirit. To be born again means we say goodbye to our former live and embrace our new life in Jesus Christ. To be born again of the spirit is to accept Jesus Christ as our Lord and Saviour.

To live the Christ life means the studying and applying the word daily. The Bible has the answers to all the problems in our world. It is up to us to study and change our world. As light of the world we need to shine in our dark world.

> "Study to show yourself approved unto God, a workman that needeth not to be ashamed, rightly dividing the Word of Truth."- 2 Tim 2:15 kjv.

Christians must study the Bible to show ourselves approved of God. It is only when we know the word that we can apply it practically and effectively. We are to make the effort to do so. By studying the word we also need to be able to rightly apply it in any given situation. We have to know the bible as the lawyer knows the law.

The level of our desire to know the world will determine how far we will get to know Jesus. Let us make the study of the Bible our lifestyle. We are blessed in our generation to have so many resources to help build us up in our faith and walk with Jesus Christ. We have these on Christian television, radio, books, DVD's and the web. Ultimately, we are blessed to have the Holy Spirit as our Helper to guide us into all truths. He is the One who reveal Jesus to us. The most important thing is to study to know the word for yourself.

Let us ask the Holy Spirit to help us understand the Word of God concerning our life. The use of daily devotional aid materials such as the "daily bread" and others can be of great help. Hiding the word of God in our heart will keep our focus right and prevent sin. King David in the Bible discovered this and wrote:

> "Your Word I have hidden in my heart, that I might not sin against You, bless are You O Lord, Teach me Your statutes. (Psalm 119.11-12)

Faith comes by hearing and hearing by the Word of God. Jesus speaks to us through reading and studying the Bible.

It is through the study that we get to know Who Jesus is and what He has already done for us. We also do get to know what he wants us to do. The more you get to know Jesus the more you want to know Him. The apostle Paul walked with Christ for many years and said, "that I may know Him." (Phil3: 10). He wanted to know Jesus more and more each day. It gets sweeter and sweeter by the day.

The Word enlightens our spiritual eyes to see the greatness of our God and His creative and saving power! We can also know how to have a wonderful fellowship with the most powerful Person in the whole universe, the Holy Spirit. There is so much in the Bible that would amaze and interest you to know.

When Christ found me and accepted me into His kingdom, the Holy Spirit helped me to study the Bible and it has never been boring, but lively and exciting. It has been a continuous life changing experience. You can experience it too!

The Word as The tool.
The Word of the Lord has been described symbolically in order to help with our understanding of what it does. As Jesus is described as the Word of God, it also mean what Jesus is when we allow Him to operate in our life. We will look at some of these to help with our study on faith and how to ignite our world.

1. The Word- Fire and Hammer

"Is not My Word like FIRE? Says the Lord, and like the HAMMER that breaks the rock in pieces? - Jeremiah 23.29

The Word of God convicts the world of sin. It convicts individuals of any wrongdoing. As fire you can use the word to refine your spiritual life. All the chaff from the devil and the old life will be burnt. We can also use the word as a hammer to shape our life to conform to that of Jesus. Let us be transformed by doing what Jesus says.

2. The Word – 'Refreshing'

God compared His spoken and written word to the coming down of rain and snow. He said:

> "For as the rain comes down, and the snow from heaven, and do not return there, but water the earth, and make it bring forth and bud, that it may give seed to the sower and bread to the eater. So shall My Word be that goes forth from My mouth it shall not RETURN TO ME VOID, but it shall accomplish what I please. And it shall prosper in the thing for which I sent it. (Isaiah 55.10-11)

Wow! What a refreshing and assuring word from God! We can only discover these truths and assurances only when we study the word of God.

If Jesus has forgiven you of all your sins, then you can walk in this life by forgiving yourself of past sins that the devil holds against you by exercising your right to that promise. We can then share the word with others to come to the saving knowledge of Christ. All these precious treasures in His word can be discovered, so start 'digging'. It is a gold mine full of treasures, and a fountain full of living waters. Start reading and study the Bible.

3. The Word – Source of Faith and Eternal Life.

"Having been born again, not of corruptible seed but incorruptible, through the word of God which lives and abides forever."-1 Peter 1.23

"So faith comes by hearing and hearing by the word of God." -Romans10.17

Once again we can only come to understand the concept of "born again" through reading and studying the word. We should desire to have great faith. The incorruptible seed is the life of the father, which is in the son (Jesus Christ) and now in us. This seed is the eternal life Jesus came to reveal to us through His Word by His death and resurrection.

4. The Word – 'For Cleansing

There is so much bad news and evil around the world in these end times as prophesied by the Bible. These include murder, hatred, envy, rejection, death, terrorism, and threat of nuclear war. These bombard our minds and have the ability to produce fear in us. We need the cleansing power of God to wipe out these thoughts and visual forms of evil we see daily. The answer to this is in His Word.

"That He might sanctify and cleanse her (the church, you and me) with the washing of water by the Word.

For our daily cleansing to conform to the image of Jesus, we must never forget to read and study the word.

5. The Word – Spiritual Food To Nourish.

a. For Baby Christians.
God has provided for all new born again Christians spiritual food in the form of 'milk', which could be easily digested to enhance spiritual growth in faith. This is described as 'sincere milk of the word'. "As new born babies desire the pure milk of the word that you may grow thereby." (1Peter2.2).

The only way new believers can grow into maturity is to study the manual of life, the Bible, to build a solid spiritual foundation that could be built on. There is no staying away from the reading and studying of the Bible.

b. Meat For Adults
"But solid food belongs to those who are full of age that is those who by reason of the use have their senses exercised to discern both good and evil."(Hebrews 5.14)

What we just read are some of the qualities expected from a maturing or matured child of God. Baby Christians after learning the basic foundations on salvation, baptism and laying on of hands are expected to grow into maturity. These are possible through knowing what the Bible says concerning all issues of life.

6. The Word – Sword Of The Spirit

The word of God is our spiritual sword for attacking and defeating the devil against his evil thoughts.

> "For the Word of God is living and powerful, and sharper than any two –edged sword, piercing even to the division of the soul and spirit and of joint and marrow, and is a discerner of the thoughts and intents of the heart -Hebrews 4.12.

We can only overcome the devil by the words of our testimony based on the infallible Word of God. His word is living and powerful and sharper than any weapon the devil has and is prepared to use against you.

You have the most powerful weapon than the world's most powerful nuclear arsenal. Use it.

7. The Word –A Lamp To Guide And More Than Gold To Enrich.

We are given a guide to our life. In the same way we read product manuals for effective usage, so we should read the Bible to live effective and holy life.

The Word will keep us on the highest alert especially in these last days as we are preparing for Christ's coming for His church. "Your word is a lamp to my feet and a light to my path" - Psalm119.105.

Let our desire for the word increase. The key to true greatness is making the Word of God your guide in all things. This is what the great men of old and those around now discovered. They used it as the standard for living. This discovery helped them to build their strong faith, which made them to do the great things we read about.

Psalm 19.7-10 is a perfect example of how rich the word of God can make us.

> "The word of the lord is perfect, converting the soul. The testimony of God is sure, making wise the simple, the statutes of the Lord, are right, rejoicing the heart, the commandment of the Lord are pure enlightening the eyes. THE FEAR OF THE LORD IS CLEAN, ENDURING FOREVER. They are more precious than gold, than much pure gold, they are sweeter than honey from the comb."

His Word is perfect and makes the simple people like the Prophets Elijah, Elisha, the apostle Peter, and tens of millions of others wise. This wisdom comes from the knowledge of God and Jesus Christ.

It has made me a wise person too compared to the time before my conversion. It brings joy to hearts and encouragement to the hurt and broken hearted.

The fear of the Lord is clean and will endure forever. It is also the beginning of wisdom. The fear of God will help us to equip ourselves in order to share the good news with anybody.

Some Effective Ways For Studying The Bible

The following are some suggestions on some effective ways on studying the Bible. You may have others, which you can add. This has helped me a lot.

1. Find yourself a study Bible with concordance and a notebook.
2. Pray and ask the Holy Spirit to help you study. Start with a book such as "John" and study chapter by chapter, exhausting it completely. Let the Holy Spirit open the scriptures to you.
3. Take some characters in the Bible and make some notes on these characters. (E.g. Samuel, Moses, Joseph, Jesus, Paul and others) Study along these lines:
    a. Their strengths, vision, purpose and mission.
    b. How they begun their faith journey with God.
    c. Their weaknesses.
    d. How they overcame such weaknesses.

  e. How they handled success and many others as the Holy Spirit reveals to you.
4. Put yourself in their position and with the help of the Holy Spirit decide what you will do in any situation.

These and other studying skills will help us to study the Bible effectively. Let the Holy Spirit help you in your study of the Word of God.

Lifestyle To Change Our World.
After equipping ourselves with the word, our lifestyle should reflect that of Jesus. In Acts 11, the lifestyle of the followers of Jesus was worth noticing. This was the first time the followers of Jesus were called Christians. Do you remember when Jesus was under trial? Peter was not too far away from Him warming himself. Someone identified him as a follower of Jesus through his lifestyle.

  Can we be identified with Jesus through our lifestyle? The Holy Spirit is our helper in living the life as followers of Jesus. By living in the spirit we demonstrate the fruit of the spirit to the world. This is the only way all will know that we are the ones who will make a change as Jesus and the early Christians did.

  We must shun sin in any form or shape. Compromise is destroying our convictions and message. If it is not faith then it must be sin.

What Jesus calls sin we must call it the same. We must walk our talk. How can we claim to be followers of Jesus when we do not love one another? We are to love Jesus by keeping His commandments.

We studied in the first Chapter that our faith in Jesus is based on love. The only way we can influence our society and change our world is to love one another and live in unity. This will be worth noticing in the society. They will also notice you bearing the fruit of the spirit.

We live in a world void of love, peace, affection, patience and longsuffering. Our demonstration of any of these will attract attention, which will bring the change needed in the world. People will like to know why that difference in you.

For us to be effective in our witness, we must be all things to all people. This is not to say we become sinners, but rather put ourselves in their shoes and share the good news of Jesus. The apostle Paul showed us how to do this:

> "For though I am free from all men, I have made myself a servant to all that I might win the more." -1 Corinthians 9: 19

Here are some of the characters Paul become:
  a. To the Jews he became a Jew.
  b. To the weak, he became weak.
  c. "To those who are without law, as without law (not being without law toward God, but

under law toward Christ), that I might win those who are without law:" -1 Cor 9:21.

In all of Paul's effort to win more to Christ, he did not loose his focus on Christ. Let our lifestyle reflect our talk and win our relatives, colleagues, friends, enemies and all to Christ. Our faith will be rewarded. Remember it is not over until Jesus says so. Your life will count and you will make a difference in your part of the world. Together we can all turn our world "upside down" and empty it of all evil and fill it with the glory of God.

Remember you may be the only Bible someone in the world will ever read. Let you life reflect on your profession as a child of God and a follower of Jesus Christ. Let your focus be on Christ only.

We will now conclude by learning some principles on how to share the good news.

-Chapter 9-

Focus on Jesus- change your world

.....looking unto Jesus, the author and finisher of *our* faith.."Heb 12:1b

Sharing The Good News.
Everything God has promised in His word belongs to anyone who has accepted Jesus as their personal Lord and Saviour. Now you will know how to exercise your right as a child of God after getting to know what God's word says about Him and you.

Our priorities can be right with the focus on Jesus. We need to know that the word of God is the power of God. There is no power strong enough to destroy what you have been given. The power and authority you have is divine.

In John 13:4-5 Jesus taught about how to be a leader by demonstrating to the disciples. This was in the washing of their feet. At first Peter resisted, as it was not normal for the leader to serve. Later he learnt from Jesus the new principle on leadership. Our lifestyle can reflect that of Jesus when we practice what is taught in this book based mainly on biblical account and experience.

Talk The Walk.
It is very crucial to first demonstrate the life of Jesus before talking about it.

Our life literally speaks about 70% of who we are or represent in our case.

Jesus always lived the life before teaching people. For example, when He wanted to teach on leadership, he demonstrated that by serving. This was when He washed the feet of the disciples as we read earlier. Jesus must be seen in you through demonstrating the works of faith by helping people. This is to emphasise on what was read in john 13 earlier.

Now let us get back to where we started. We have received the ingredients to help us focus on Jesus to share the good news. We can now talk to people about Jesus. We must be ready.

Sacrifice And The Good News.
Jesus sacrificed Himself by coming to die on the cross to save all of us. He exchanged His crown of glory for thorns!! The creator of the universe was denied water and dignity when He needed them.

He was vulnerable as a baby. How can the creator become part of creation and be subject to it laws? We can talk about this exchange and Jesus' sacrifice in volumes upon volumes of books.

The bottom line is that He did that because of the reality and devastating nature of our eternal punishment due to disobedience. His love for you and me took Him to the cross. He made it to the cross and finished the redemptive work for mankind. Salvation is now open to all.

Jesus sacrificed for you and me. Are we prepared to do the same by introducing Him to our family, friends and everyone?

We are now the representatives of Jesus who should carry on with the work of Jesus. We have been empowered and given all the necessary tools needed. Let us take some risk to save the world.

Contact with Good News.
Naturally good news is shared. Even the most selfish person reluctantly may decide to share his or her good news at the end in one-way or the other. A new parent comes out and shouts to the family and friends "it's a boy or girl"!! Someone who buys a new car or house would like to share the good news. It is just normal.

Let us look at the effect on the good news of Christ on people starting from the call of the first disciples as given by the New Testament gospel writers.

Andrew (John 1): One day John the Baptist saw Jesus walk past and said "Behold the Lamb of God." The two disciples of John left him and started following Jesus. He asked them what they wanted. They asked where Jesus was staying. One of the two was Andrew.

This is what Andrew did on finding the Messiah. "He first found his own brother Simon, and said to him, "we have found the Messiah" (which is translated, the Christ.) And He brought him to Jesus."- (Verse 41-42)

Isn't that amazing? He first found his brother and shared the good news about the Messiah. He did not stop there. Secondly, Andrew brought Simon Peter to Jesus. This is how we should do it. When Jesus saved me, I did not keep quite but first shared it with my parents, cousins, nieces, nephews and friends. Unfortunately I lost some friends along the way too as I was no longer doing the same old stuff with them and their unwillingness to consider looking into living this new life of hope and change.

Philip: "The following day Jesus wanted to go to Galilee, and He found Philip and He said to him, "follow Me," Philip was from the same town as Andrew and Peter. Philip found Nathanael and said to him, "we have found Him of whom Moses in the law, and also the prophets, wrote-Jesus of Nazareth, the son of Joseph. Come and see." -John 1:43-45

Philip couldn't contain the joy. He shared it by taking action as well just as Andrew did. It was as though he said to Nathanael come and experience Jesus for yourself.

Samaritan woman: An interesting story unfolds in John chapter 4, when Jesus left Judea because of certain accusations and went back to Galilee. He had to go through Samaria. Jesus came to a city in Samaria called Sychar, which was near a plot of land that Jacob gave to his son Joseph.

He was so tired that He sat at one of Jacob's well at that site to relax. A Samaritan woman came to draw water. Jesus asked for a drink of water because His disciples have gone to town to buy food. The woman's response was that of one in shock: "you are a Jew and I am a Samaritan woman, how can you ask me for a drink? –Verse 9. (For Jews dis not associate with Samaritans in those days.)

If this was some of us on trying to share some good news, the reaction may have been different such as even the end of that conversation. bye, bye, Lady, I was only trying to get you saved!! With Jesus things were different. The conversation now progressed from racial differences unto respect when she addressed Jesus as "Sir". Jesus introduced the living waters, which this woman was interested.

Jesus then asked her to go home and call her husband. The answer was that she had none. Jesus told her everything about her life including living with someone else's husband. Trust now gave way for respect and reverence. She perceived Jesus to be a prophet. Then the conversation progressed further into worship. The woman then said what she knew the Messiah would do when He comes. Jesus then revealed to her who He was, that Messiah she was talking about.

This is the effect of that message on seeing the Messiah.
"Then leaving her water jar, the woman went back to the town and said to the people,

"come, and see a man Who told me everything I ever did. Could this be the Christ? They came out of the city and made their way toward Him.- verse 28-30. Now here is the greatest part.

> "Many of the Samaritans from that town believed in him because of the woman's testimony. "he told me everything I ever did." So when the Samaritans came to him, they urged Him to stay with them, and He stayed two days. And because of His word many more became believers. They said to the woman, "We no longer believe just because of what you said; now we have heard for ourselves, and we know that this man really is the Saviour of the world."- John 4:39-42 NIV

Did you see how the conversation progressed from racial tension unto salvation for many in that town/city? This story summarises all what we have studied in this book. We are the representatives of Christ who need to introduce Him to a dying world. We do that through our character and preaching. I call this woman the "Samaritan evangelist"! You can also be your "town or city evangelist".

She left her water jar when she met the Saviour. Her priorities changed immediately.
Salvation and the kingdom of God now became first priority before any other thing. She did not keep the word and experience to herself and felt cool about it.

She knew exactly who needed to hear the message of salvation from the Saviour. She went extreme to tell the whole city!

We studied in various Chapters that people need to experience Jesus for themselves. That is what the people in the town did and testified to it. They were grateful that the woman shared her testimony, which they believed. But now they believed because they had a first hand experience with Jesus Christ for themselves. Something no amount of description could explain it.

Called To Be A Witness.
We have been called to be witnesses. The difference here is that our total life must reflect that of Jesus. This is the reason why I started teaching on lifestyle, reading, studying and preaching the word. This will help us live more and more like Jesus. The effect will be the same it had on all who came into contact with Him.

You are not a Christian called to witness. You are the witness everywhere you find yourself. Please never forget that. There is a plastic wristband and other artifacts with the inscription "W.W.J.D?" –What Will Jesus Do. In every situation remember Who you are representing. As an ambassador of Christ, you must represent Him in the same way He would like you to do.

Cross the line- The Crown Awaits You.
The faith journey will be unproductive if we fall on the wayside without finishing the race.

Our focus is on Jesus the author and FINISHER of our faith. In the account of the faith heroes in Hebrews 11, they all died or finished well in faith. It is only those who finish and win races that receive the gold. This could be in athletics or any other sport discipline. This is the same for our faith with the best reward that cannot be compared to anything on earth.

The apostle Paul was able to complete his faith journey. He fought the good fight of faith and did the work of an evangelist. He said, "for I am already been poured out like a drink offering, and the time has come for my departure, I have fought the good fight of faith, I have finished the race, I have kept the faith. Now there is in store for me the crown of righteousness, which the Lord, the righteous Judge, will award to me on that day-and not only to me, but also to those who have longed for his appearing." -2 Timothy 4:6-8.)

This is my prayer for everyone. Focus on Jesus like Paul, fight the good fight of faith, win souls by sharing your own testimony of how you came to know Jesus, keep the faith and end in faith. Your crown will be waiting you in heaven as Paul said. Jesus is coming sooner than we thought.

Reference

Focus definition; Apple McIntosh system dictionary "Aa" version 2.2.1

Patterson, David. The four causes of blurry photos, and how to fix them.
http://www.digitalphotosecrets.com/tip/129/the-top-4-causes-of-blurry-photos-and-how-to-fix-them/

Sproule, John. The Problem of the Mustard Seed. Grace Theological Journal 1.1 (1980) 37-42

What is the meaning of the Greek work *dunamis* in the Bible. https://www.gotquestions.org/dunamis-meaning.html

Made in the USA
Coppell, TX
06 June 2023